THINK IT OUT

by Libby Selman

E. J. ARNOLD & SON LIMITED LEEDS

ISBN 0-560-01039 X

Contents

1 Hardness 7

2 The Size of Your Shoes 9

3 Matching Partners 12

4 Noise 14

5 The Prisoner's Dilemma 17

6 The Age of the Population 19

7 Murder 21

8 Crop Rotation 23

9 Identifying Animal Tracks 25

10 A Place in the Boat 28

11 Cloth and Clothes 31

12 Repairs Budget 34

13 Iron and Steel 37

14 The Bilharzia Worm 41

15 Roads in Winter 44

16 Methods of Grinding Grain 46

17 The Mayan System of Numbers 48

18 Canal Locks 51

    Answers 54

Acknowledgements

E. J. Arnold wish to express thanks
to the following for their kind
assistance in the preparation of certain units:

Clarks Shoe Manufacturers (Unit 2)
Noise Abatement Society (Unit 4)
Yorkshire Post Newspapers (Unit 4)
Controller, HMSO (Unit 6)
Wool Industries Research Association (Unit 11)

Introduction

The reading passages in this book and the activities associated with them are designed for use as supplementary material at lower intermediate level and above. They are intended to give practice in oral, reading and writing skills in English through the completion of challenging and interesting language exercises.

The units were first used with students intending to go on to further studies using English as the medium of instruction, and aimed to provide lessons where the language itself was not the focus of attention. Although language is learned or revised as an inevitable part of the working out of the tasks, the emphasis of the lessons is on reading for content and meaning rather than the analysis or appreciation of linguistic form. For teachers who wish to exploit the language of particular units more fully (say, the use of contrast markers in 'Animal Tracks' or the conditional forms in 'The Prisoner's Dilemma') it is suggested that this could best be done after task-completion.

The units in the book are of two types:

1   Task-completion   These comprise a range of informative general knowledge passages. The tasks based on them take a variety of forms but all involve careful reading and comprehension of a text, the extracting of information from it, and the re-use of it in a different context. The interpretation and use of non-verbal information from diagrams plays an important part in many of these units.

2   Problem-solving   A number of units present the readers with a problem to solve. Once again, careful reading of the text is required, followed by an assessment of the information given and the preparation of a coherent solution to the problem.

The units are arranged in a rough order of difficulty, taking into consideration the complexity of both the reading passages and the related tasks. However, it is not intended that the teacher or students should necessarily work through the units consecutively. Technical or semi-technical language relevant to particular topics has not been glossed, in the belief that students should be encouraged where possible to use the contextual clues and accompanying diagrams to infer the meaning of unfamiliar words.

The material in the book is suitable for use in a number of ways and may be recommended as supplementary reading and writing practice for students working alone. An answer section is included at the back of the book for self-correction of the exercises and suggested solutions to the problems. In class, both types of unit may be done by students working individually or co-operatively. The problem-solving type is particularly suitable for investigation and discussion with students in small groups or pairs.

1 HARDNESS

Hardness is not strength. Many hard materials are brittle; in other words, they break easily — for example, glass or dry twigs are hard, but easily broken.

Hardness is the ability of a material to resist scratching. For instance, steel will scratch or even cut wood, so steel is harder than wood; but steel will not scratch diamond, so we say that diamond is harder than steel.

Diamond, in fact, is the hardest natural substance; borazon, a man-made material, is even harder.

A German scientist, Friedrich Mohs, composed a scale of hardness, which is called Mohs' scale. This uses the numbers 1 to 10; 1 is the softest end of the scale, 10 the hardest.

MOHS' SCALE	
	name of material
1	talc
2	gypsum
3	calcite
4	fluorite
5	apatite
6	feldspar
7	quartz
8	topaz
9	corundum
10	diamond

A material that can be scratched by quartz (hardness 7) but not by feldspar (hardness 6) is given a value between 6 and 7. A fingernail is about hardness 2; a shiny new one penny piece is about 3; a steel knife is about 6.

There are also more accurate ways to measure hardness. A pyramid-shaped diamond can be pressed into the surface of the material, after which the size of the dent in the material is measured. The smaller the dent, the harder the material; the larger the dent, the softer the material.

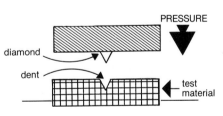

Using the information in the above passage, answer the following questions:

1   Fill in the blanks:
   (a)   _____ is the hardest substance found naturally.
   (b)   _____ is the hardest known substance.

2 *Brittle* means:
(a) strong, (b) weak, (c) soft or (d) easily broken.

3 Following the example in the passage which reads, 'steel is harder than wood', make sentences comparing these materials:
(a) fingernail/hard/wax
(b) steel/soft/diamond
(c) diamond/soft/borazon.

4 Using Mohs' scale, complete these sentences:
(a) Window glass, which can be scratched by feldspar but not by apatite, has a hardness value of_____.
(b) An old coin, which can scratch gypsum but not calcite, has a hardness value of_____.

5 In the diagram, (a), (b) and (c) have all been dented with a diamond:

Which test material is the hardest?

6 Fill in the missing words:

hard	hardness
	strength
soft	

7 Say which of the following statements are true and which are false:
(a) Your fingernail cannot scratch a new penny.
(b) A steel knife cannot cut quartz.
(c) Diamond can scratch glass.

8 Find a verb in the passage which completes sentence (b) so that (a) and (b) mean the same:
(a) Steel cannot be scratched by calcite.
(b) Steel_____scratching by calcite.

9 Using objects which you can easily find around you, and which are made from different materials, compose
(i) your own list of materials which are
(a) hard but brittle
(b) hard but strong
(ii) your own scale of hardness.

2　THE SIZE OF YOUR SHOES

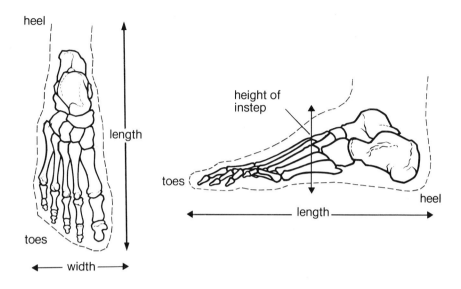

The size of the shoes you should buy depends on the bones of your feet, which you can see in the illustration. The correct size is important — for comfort, obviously, and also for health. Shoes that are the wrong size can damage feet, especially for growing children.

To choose shoes that fit perfectly, you need to know how long your feet are (the length from heel to toe) and how wide (the width of the widest part). The height of your instep can also be important; if you have a high instep you may need wider shoes.

Length is the most important measurement for finding shoe size. But, unfortunately, even when you know how long your feet are, you can still have problems, because there are several different systems of labelling sizes — British, American and Continental, for example.

Here is a way to find out your British shoe size. It isn't exact, but it's quite interesting to try. Remember, one of your feet may be longer than the other. Measure the length of your *longer* foot in centimetres. For adults, multiply this number by 6, divide by 5 and subtract 23. Your answer should be a number from 1 to 10, which is your shoe size (unless you have more than usually large feet!). For children, multiply the number by 6, divide by 5 and subtract 10½. Children's shoes can go up to size 13.

This table shows how the British sizes compare with American and Continental sizes.

ADULTS				CHILDREN	
British	Continental	American Women	Men	British	Continental
1	33	2½	For men,	10	28
2	34	3½	try 1 size	11	29
3	35 or 36	4½	larger	12	30 or 31
4	37	5½	than the	13	32
5	38	6½	usual UK		
6	39	7½	size. For	For children, in
7	40 or 41	8½	example,	most cases there
8	42	9½	UK 6 may	are half-sizes
9	43	10½	be US size	between the lengths
10	44	11½	6½ or 7	in the UK system

Questions on length and size

1 Mary wears British size 3 shoes. Susan has longer feet and wears British size 7. Mary's daughter Anne wears British children's size 12. Mary, Susan and Anne all have the same problem if they buy Continental shoes. What is it?

2 A man who is used to British size shoes has to add ½ or 1 to his size when he buys American shoes. How much does a woman who is used to British size shoes have to add to her size when she buys American shoes?

For every size of shoe, there are different widths. Again, unfortunately, there are different systems, as shown in the following table:

	WOMEN British	American	MEN British	American
narrowest	AA	AAAA	1	A
	A	AAA	2	B
	B	AA	3	C
	C	A	4	D
	D	B	5	E
	E	C	6	F
	EE or F	D	7	G
widest	G	E	8	H

Questions on width

3 If you wear British EE fitting (women's), can you wear American E? Will the shoes fit perfectly, or be too tight or too loose?

4 If you wear American D fitting (men's), what width fitting do you need for British shoes?

For the following question, use the information on both length and width:

5 Can you help the Carters to buy shoes? The Carters are an American family visiting England, and they all need new shoes after walking round looking at all the tourist spots. Mr Hank Carter wears American size 11½, H width. Mrs Marilyn Carter wears American 5½ AAA. They don't know the size for their son Junior, because his feet keep growing — but his longer foot is 18 cm long. What sizes of British shoes must they buy?

And lastly, some interesting information:

6 The tallest man ever reliably documented wore size 37 AA shoes (US); can you work out how long his feet were?

7 It pays to choose your shoes carefully!

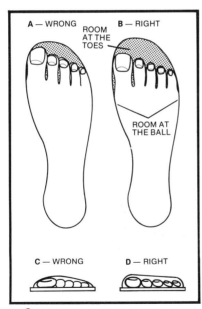

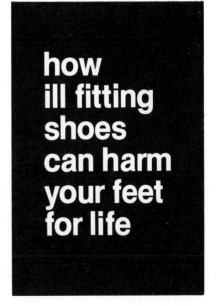

how ill fitting shoes can harm your feet for life

Clarks

3 MATCHING PARTNERS

Richard and Mary are two people who both want to marry, but haven't got anyone suitable to marry. Both of them saw the following advertisement in a newspaper:

> **MODERN MATCHING**
>
> Find a friend or lover or husband or wife! Find your perfect partner through our computer matching service! Fill in the form below and send, with a recent colour photograph and a cheque for only £10, to Modern Matching. We will send you the name and address of your perfect partner!

Richard and Mary carefully filled in the forms, sent them to Modern Matching, and each received the other's name, address and telephone number. They contacted each other, and agreed to meet in a restaurant. After the meeting, they both wrote to Modern Matching to complain that there must be something wrong with the computer.

Compare the forms they filled in and make a list of the ways in which Richard and Mary were badly matched.

MODERN MATCHING	
Fill in your *own* characteristics on the left side of the page. Fill in the characteristics you want your *partner* to have on the right side of the page.	
name *Mary Reed*	
age 33	age 30-35
sex *female*	sex *male*
nationality *American*	nationality *doesn't matter*
occupation *journalist*	occupation *doesn't matter*
height 5'7"	height *doesn't matter, but*
build *rather heavy*	build *I like big men*
colouring *dark*	colouring *doesn't matter*
religion *no religion (atheist)*	religion *doesn't matter*
politics *left-wing*	politics *doesn't matter*
marital status *divorced (3 years ago)*	marital status *doesn't matter*
attitude to children *I have 2 already – no more!*	attitude to children *must like mine and want no more*
car owner? *yes*	car owner? *yes*
smoker? *yes, 40 a day*	smoker? *doesn't matter*
interests etc. *meeting people, parties, theatre, political meetings*	interests etc. *anything. NB– he must look after the children if I have to work late*

MODERN MATCHING

Fill in your *own* characteristics on the left side of the page. Fill in the characteristics you want your *partner* to have on the right side of the page.

name Richard Briggs

age 30	age 20-28
sex male	sex female
nationality British	nationality not American
occupation bank clerk	occupation doesn't matter
height 5'4"	height under 5'4"
build thin	build slim. not fat
colouring fair	colouring fair-haired
religion Church of England	religion doesn't matter
politics no interest	politics doesn't matter
marital status unmarried [bachelor]	marital status must be free to marry
attitude to children I love children I want four	attitude to children must love children
car owner? no	car owner? doesn't matter
smoker? no	smoker? non-smoker
interests etc. gardening I'm very shy and don't like parties or crowds	interests etc. I want a quiet, home-loving woman

Fill in a similar form yourself, with the qualities you would want in a partner. Do you think the form above asks the right questions? How would you change it?

What's your opinion about a firm like Modern Matching and the service it offers? Do you think it can work?

Write a letter of complaint from Richard or Mary to Modern Matching, explaining how badly matched you were.

How do you think *you* would like either Richard or Mary?

4 NOISE

Noise, to the scientist, is any sound made by an *irregular* pattern of sound waves. Music, in contrast, is sound with a *regular* waveform.

But the word 'noise', in everyday language, usually means sound that we find unpleasant — and often, that unpleasantness takes the form of *loudness.*

Intensity	db	Typical sounds
x 1	0	Threshold of hearing
x 10	10	Leaves rustling in the wind
x 100	20	Quiet country lane
x 1 000	30	Tick of watch; whisper
x 10 000	40	Quiet office; quiet conversation
x 100 000	50	Inside average home
x 1 000 000	60	Normal conversation at 3 feet
x 10 000 000	70	Busy street; building noise
x 100 000 000	80	**DANGER LEVEL** Noisy office; alarm clock; inside small car
x 1 000 000 000	90	Heavy truck; underground train
x 10 000 000 000	100	Inside train compartment when door is slammed; food blender at 2 feet
x 100 000 000 000	110	Pop group at 4 feet; power mower at 4 feet; motor horn at 20 feet
x 1 000 000 000 000	120	**THRESHOLD OF PAIN** Jet aircraft at 500 feet; inside boiler factory
x 10 000 000 000 000	130	Jet engine at 100 feet; air-raid siren; pneumatic riveter
x 100 000 000 000 000	140	
x 1 000 000 000 000 000	150	Sound at speech frequencies can burn the skin
x 10 000 000 000 000 000	160	
x 100 000 000 000 000 000	170	
x 1 000 000 000 000 000 000	180	**LETHAL LEVEL**
x 10 000 000 000 000 000 000	190	
x 100 000 000 000 000 000 000	200	Noise weapon

To measure loudness we use a unit called the *decibel (db)*. The loudest sounds we encounter may have an intensity of a million million times that of the faintest sound we can hear. To take this into account, the scale of decibels is a logarithmic scale — in other words, for every increase of ten decibels, the intensity of the sound increases ten *times.*

This method of measuring will become clearer after study of the rough table of loudness values above. This is of course subject to a great deal of variation — the people on your particular train may close the compartment doors very quietly — but it serves as a good example of the dangers of loud noise which we face every day.

Most people hear less well as they grow older, and many become deaf in old age. But people who work in noisy conditions for a long period run the risk of deafness *before* they grow old. Put the following jobs in order of the risk of deafness. 1 will be the highest risk, because of the noisiest conditions, 6 will be the lowest risk (in this group).

A   an office-worker surrounded by people typing
B   a person keeping crowds off stage during a rock concert
C   an aeroplane mechanic testing engines
D   an engineer working in a boilermakers
E   a shipyard worker using a pneumatic riveter
F   a traffic policeman at a busy junction

In the following paragraph, a symbol is inserted at each point where a noise level (expressed in db) has been omitted. Substitute the approximate number for each symbol.

'I work in a quiet office (G). Usually, the loudest noise comes through the open window from the building-site (H), and people in the office talk very quietly (I). But the train to work in the morning is very noisy because of all the compartment doors slamming (J) at every station, and when I change to the Underground (K) it's not much better.
'At lunchtime yesterday I walked down to the park for some air. The road to the park is busy, with heavy traffic (L), but the park itself is perfect. I could hear the rustling of leaves on the trees (M), birds singing, and young lovers whispering together (N). I sat down on a seat by the path. Unfortunately, I sat next to a young woman with a child who started to scream so loudly it was almost painful to hear (O), so I went back to the office for some peace and quiet.'

Sounds under 20 db can be described as *very faint;*
                    from 20 to 30   *faint;*
                    from 30 to 60   *moderate;*
                    from 60 to 90   *loud;*
                    from 90 to 100   *very loud;*
                    over 100   *painfully or dangerously loud.*

Give some examples of sounds that you consider are (P) faint, (Q) moderate, (R) very loud.
For example: a mouse squeaking (faint)
                    a teacher explaining to a student (moderate)
                    a powerful motor bike (very loud).

Leeds probe into disco noise danger

SATURDAY NIGHT HEADACHE

By HELEN SCOTT

As Saturday Night Fever sweeps Leeds, scientists are warning about the dangers of exposure to disco noise.

And the Noise Advisory Council is sponsoring a research project at Leeds Polytechnic into whether disco noise can damage the hearing of young people.

The survey is being carried out by the Environmental Health Department at the Poly, has been going on for over a year and is due to report next January. A team has been taking noise tests in discos in West Yorkshire.

Mrs. Anne Gregory, a research assistant on the project, said Leeds discos were fairly responsible.

EAR PLUGS

"Evidence suggests that in certain premises there may be a danger risk but generally there is not much risk unless a young person goes every night." she said.

"We are just trying to work out what suitable noise levels are by looking at attendance patterns of youngsters — the highest level we recorded was 124 decibels at a punk rock concert but the average noise level in a disco is about 95 which is acceptable.

Mr. Derek Smith, manager of the Upstairs Downstairs club in Armley, Leeds, believed live concerts could cause hearing damage, but not discos.

"We do not have the music very loud in this club because I don't like it noisy."

"One of my engineers has just finished working on some live concerts in London and he did them with ear plugs in. I would think the decibel rating in Upstairs Downstairs is about 80."

In 1974 Leeds City Council imposed a noise limit of 96 decibels for concerts in the Town Hall.

A spokesman for the Environmental Health Department said: "We decided not to implement this ban — we had a new look at the problem and officers decided it would not be fair to impose any limit until the results of the survey at the Poly are published. Then we will review the situation."

5 THE PRISONER'S DILEMMA

It is the day after the military takeover of power in your country. The elected government has been totally defeated. You and your best friend, Lee, have never taken an active interest in politics, but you are both students and you know that many of your student friends have been arrested or have simply 'disappeared'.

At 9.30 in the evening there is a noise at your door and two heavily-armed soldiers burst in, arrest you and take you away in a closed van.

Now you are alone in a cell and no-one knows where you are. You are understandably terrified by what has happened, and the noise of boots in the corridor outside your cell does not make you feel any better.

A military officer enters the room. He tells you that your friend Lee has also been arrested and is in another cell. The officer wants you to sign the following 'confession':

> We confess that we worked secretly in the student movement to support the Evil Masters of the old government.
> We will now co-operate with the military powers who have liberated our country, and we will reveal all our secret information and the names of our comrades, in the interests of all the people of this glorious new republic.
>
> SIGNED.....................................
>
> DATE.......................................

You read the confession quickly and tell the officer that this isn't true; you and Lee have done nothing and have no information.

'That's what they all say — at first!' he replies. 'You must understand that we personally are not too interested in whether you are innocent or guilty.

'Let me explain the situation. Your friend Lee has the same confession on the table in front of him and we are waiting for him to sign too.

'If only one of you confesses, the confessor will be released and used as an example to encourage others to confess — but the one who does not confess will be tortured.

'If both of you confess, we will exile you. You can't stay here and will never be allowed to return, but you can choose any other country to go to.

'If neither of you confesses, you will both disappear to one of our work camps in a place no-one knows about.

'Now, will you confess?'

'How will I know if Lee has confessed or not?' you ask.

'You will not know.'

The officer leaves you for ten minutes to think about your answer. What are you going to do? You have to think quickly. Here are some questions that you must consider to make the problem clearer:

1   What is the best possible result for both you and Lee?

2   How can you get the best possible result?

3   What happens if you don't confess and Lee does?

4   What is the second-best result for both you and Lee? Why? How do you achieve this result?

5   What happens if you confess and Lee doesn't?

6   If you don't care what happens to Lee will it be easier for you to answer?

7   If you believe you must tell the truth always, can you confess? What is the risk if you take the decision not to confess?

8   The military officer is returning along the corridor. You can hear his boots on the stone floor as he approaches your cell. What *are* you going to do?

6   THE AGE OF THE POPULATION

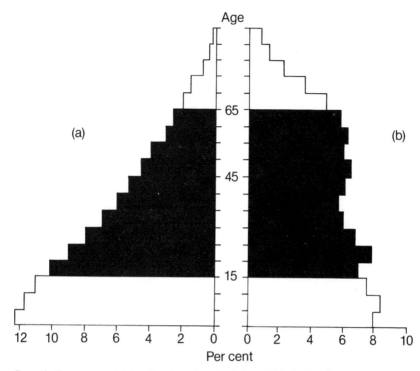

Population pyramid for England and Wales (1891/1971). (a) 1891 (both sexes); (b) 1971 (both sexes).

This population 'pyramid' compares the age of the population in England and Wales in 1891 (a) with that of England and Wales in 1971 (b). Some sociologists say that countries which display this type of movement in age patterns have the problem of an ageing population; that is, there are many old people and relatively few young or middle-aged people to support them. We should examine the pyramid more closely before discussing the problem.

Age is shown in five-year blocks on the <u>vertical axis</u> (which runs from top to bottom); the percentage of the population in each of these age groups is shown on the <u>horizontal axis</u> (which runs from side to side). Use the following questions as a guide to understanding the pyramid.

1   What is the greatest age that can be shown on this pyramid? Do many people live to a greater age than this?

2   In 1891, what % (percentage) of the population was over 85? And what % of the population was under 5?

3 So, in 1891, were there a *few* more young children than old people — or *far* more?

4 In 1891, was a greater or smaller % of the population under 15 than in 1971?

5 In 1891, was a greater or smaller % of the population over 65 than in 1971?

6 What was the largest age group in 1891? Was it the same group as the largest in 1971? Are these age groups very different or nearly the same, (i) in age, (ii) in % of the total?

7 On the pyramid, the 15 to 65 age group is shaded much darker than the under 15 or over 65 age groups. This is done in order to show that the 15 to 65 group is importantly different — in what way?

8 Within the 15 to 65 age group, which was the largest group in 1891? And in 1971?

According to some sociologists, it is when the two dependent groups (that is, non-employed people of under 15 and over 65) added together are nearly as large as the working group that countries have problems. This was not the situation in England and Wales in 1891 or in 1971, but if it should ever occur, what problems can you imagine it might cause?

Let's imagine that the population pyramid for the year 2000 shows that a great % of the people are over 65 in your country. What answers do you suggest to the problems this might create? For example, do you want to encourage your people to have more children or fewer?

7 MURDER

```
Athelstane Bugle
est. 1890
LOCAL RESIDENT FOUND
DEAD AT HOME
Foul play suspected
```

So, Miss Pat Pond has been murdered. Her coffee was poisoned. She was very rich and her will said that her money must be divided between her four nephews, Alan, Bob, Colin and Dan.

The police have all four nephews on their list of suspects. Alan is a chemist and sells poisonous substances. Bob is known as a gambler and people say that he needs money to pay back some big debts. Colin has always hated his aunt since she refused to lend him the money to stop him going out of business a few years ago. Dan admits that he actually made his aunt's coffee that night at 7.30 pm. Miss Pond was found dead at 11 pm.

All the nephews will be very much richer when their aunt's money is shared out between them. But first there is the matter of the poisoned coffee to clear up.

Here are the statements made to the police by the nephews and other relatives and friends:

Dan: 'My mum asked me to take some flowers to Aunt Pat so I went with my new girlfriend, Emma, on the way to the cinema. Aunt Pat asked me to make her a cup of coffee, so I did. But I hurried off with Emma as soon as I had made it. We wanted to see ''Monster Movie'' at the cinema and it began at exactly 7.40. It must have been about 7.30 when we left the house. I never went back.'

Colin: 'I never go to Aunt Pat's house. At 7.30 last night I was watching ''Monster Movie'' at the cinema.'

Bob: 'Colin and I went to Aunt Pat's house early yesterday afternoon to borrow some money. She refused, just like she always did. So we went to Alan's shop to borrow some money from him. He refused too. I had to spend the evening watching TV with Mum because I didn't have any money to go out.'

Alan: 'I never go to my aunt's house. Bob and Colin came to my shop yesterday afternoon. They wanted to borrow some money as usual. I refused. They're always asking me for money — I don't know why they can't get themselves decent jobs.
I was busy mixing some medicine when they called, so I had to leave them alone in the shop for a few minutes. As for yesterday evening, I spent it in the pub. Ask the barman.'

Jane Lake (mother of Alan, Bob, Colin and Dan): 'Dan is the only one who really likes his aunt so I sent him with the flowers on the way to the cinema. He's a nice boy, but he seems to have changed a lot since he started going out with that Emma Rivers.
Anyway, he came home really late after "Monster Movie" and when I asked him, "Why are you so late?" he just said, "Sorry, Mum, I couldn't take the flowers to Aunt Pat till after the film. I was late and we were in a hurry."
Bob was watching TV with me, but I didn't see Alan or Colin yesterday. They don't come and see me very much these days but I can't believe they would do a thing like this.'

Emma Rivers: 'Dan and I took the flowers to his aunt about 7.30, and then we ran to the cinema to get there for the start at 7.40. After "Monster Movie" we went to my house and so Dan was late going home. I saw his brother, Colin, about 7.35 when we were running to the cinema, but he didn't say hello.
It's horrible all this about Dan's aunt, but we'll be very glad of the money — we're hoping to get married soon, you see!'

Dr Travers (police doctor): 'There is no doubt in my mind that Miss Pond was poisoned between 7.30 and 8.30 last night. The poison was in the milk which she added to her coffee.'

So who *is* the murderer? Who had a motive for putting the poison in Miss Pond's milk? Here are some points you should consider:

1 Find two statements made by Colin to the police which could be lies. How do you know that they may not be true?

2 Is Dan lying to the police or to his mother? Has he any reasons for not telling his mother the truth?

3 Who do you think committed the murder? How did he (or she) get the poison? What was his/her alibi (if any)?

4 Could two (or more) of the brothers be responsible for the murder?

5 Describe the murderer's actions for the whole day on which the murder happened.

8 CROP ROTATION IN THE VEGETABLE GARDEN

A British gardener with a large enough vegetable garden usually tries to grow a variety of crops. The main crops are:

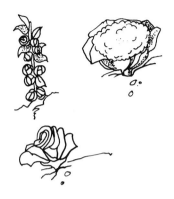

greens (cabbage, cauliflower and others)

potatoes

other root crops (such as carrots, turnips, beetroots)

and miscellaneous vegetables such as peas, beans, onions and leeks.

If he plans to grow a lot of potatoes — say, enough to supply a family throughout the year — he should follow a 4-year crop rotation plan. There are several reasons for this.

For one thing, each crop will take from the ground a larger proportion of some plant foods than of others — so, if the crop on a piece of land is frequently changed, less fertilizer is needed to restore the balance of plant foods.

More important, plants can be affected by a number of diseases; if the same crops are always in the same place they are more likely to be affected by a disease.

Finally, pests, such as the various caterpillars which eat greens, will increase in number if their food plants are always in the same place.

A simpler rotation will be safe if fewer potatoes are wanted, but the following example is best for a large crop. Generally, a good vegetable garden will be in a sunny position, and lines of vegetables will run from north to south (as far as possible) so that each plant gets a similar amount of sunshine.

In the first year, half the ground is used for potatoes. The other half is divided into two, with root crops in one part and miscellaneous vegetables in the other. Potatoes are ready to be lifted and eaten in summer, and greens take their place and stay in the ground over the winter.

In the second year, the two groups — roots and miscellaneous vegetables — will change over to the ground that was used for potatoes and greens.

In the third year, the roots and miscellaneous vegetables will go back to their original half of the garden *but* their positions will be different: the part used by roots in the first year will be used by peas, beans, onions etc., and vice versa.

The fourth year is like the second, except that again the roots and miscellaneous vegetables will take each other's positions.

In every year, potatoes and greens can share ground because they are in the ground at different seasons.

With this four-year cycle, potatoes and greens will be in the same ground only in alternate years, and all other crops will be on the same site only once in four years.

This crop rotation can easily be shown in simple diagrams. Draw a diagram of the garden in four consecutive years, using the vegetable symbols to illustrate it, and provide a key. Don't forget to show where North and South are. Then compose a simple warning for gardeners, telling them why they should rotate their crops, which will be printed on the back of vegetable seed packets. It should be short and clear.

9   IDENTIFYING ANIMAL TRACKS

Tracks are the marks made on soft ground by the feet of animals. Most animal feet consist of 3 parts — the claws, toes, and ball of the foot.

claws

toes

ball

But there are variations which enable us to identify the animal that made the tracks.

A dog's tracks are easily distinguished from a cat's: while a dog's claws make marks in front of its toeprints, a cat's claws do not touch the ground when it is walking or running, because it can *retract* them, i.e. draw them in. Both dogs and cats have four toeprints.

It is more difficult to tell a dog's track from a fox's, because both have four toe and claw marks. However, the marks of a fox's toes and the balls of its feet are nearly circular, whereas the ball of a dog's foot makes triangular marks. Also, the ball of a dog's foot makes deeper marks than a fox's. But if there is a whole line of footprints, the difference is obvious: a fox always steps in its own footmarks and so leaves a single straight line of equally spaced marks — a dog's feet leave a zigzag line of double marks.

A badger's tracks are longer than a dog's and there are five toe and claw marks. One footmark half-covers another, and the line is zigzag, not straight.

An otter is also five-toed, but as it is a swimmer its back feet are webbed (there is skin joining the toes); this can be seen in the tracks.

The <u>weasel</u> is five-toed too, but it makes separate claw marks — unlike the otter, whose claws and toes make a joint mark. And weasel tracks are obvious, because they form a series of squares.

On this page are the tracks of the dog, cat, fox, badger, otter and weasel. Using the information above, decide which are which.

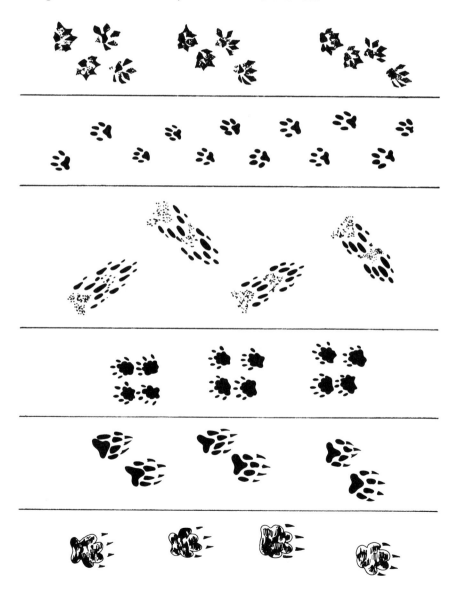

After you have completed this and looked up the answers, do the following exercise also.

Here are illustrations of various members of the cat family. Choose a few of the words and phrases supplied (and any others you may think of), and make statements comparing and contrasting these animals, either in writing or verbally.

For ideas on how to do this, look back at the passage to see how it was done for animal tracks.

similar	easily	while	distinguish . . . from . . .
different	however	tell . . . from . . .
	a lot	whereas	distinguish between . . .
obvious	a little	but	tell . . . apart
	slightly	likewise	
both	completely	as for	
also	exactly	on the other	
	(not) quite	hand	

10   A PLACE IN THE BOAT

Firstly, play this game as if you were the only person who will take the decisions. Then compare *your* solutions with those of someone else, or several others, who have decided what *they* would do.

The game shows people's reactions to an impossible situation — a situation where you cannot find any good answer. But you have to 'survive'. A 'survivor' will break a lot of normal rules of behaviour. It's interesting to compare

(i)   what dishonesty or murder different 'players' will consider;

(ii) how *long* people take to decide what to do (because a real 'survivor' would have to act quickly).

Your only chance is to escape by boat!

```
497216
JWTX YY47211      TX NO 471

ATTN ALL PERSONNEL

ARMED INVASION IMMINENT
EVACUATE IMMEDIATELY
```

The war in your country is getting nearer every day. All the soldiers of your army have disappeared and the invading enemy is now within a stone's throw of your town. It is an important town on the coast and by tomorrow the enemy soldiers will reach it and take over the port. You know they will destroy the town and kill the people, and if you stay there you will have no chance of surviving.
However, you have bought a small fishing boat with money you collected from nine other people. It's stocked with enough food, water and fuel to get ten people across the sea to safety. The boat is waiting hidden on a quiet beach from which you will all leave tonight at 11.00 p.m.
At least, that's your plan. At 8 p.m. your brother, who is one of the ten, arrives at your house in a panic.
"They cheated us when they sold us that boat!" he cries. "It can't carry ten people — it isn't strong enough. It's too full of food, the fuel's too heavy and the engine's too old. Please believe me — you know I've always worked with boats. Ten people will be too many — we shall all drown. The boat can only take eight."
Your brother has been a fisherman all his life and you know that what he says must be true. Now you both have the terrible job of deciding who to leave behind. Two people must be left if the other eight are going to survive.
Remember, they've all paid you for a place in the boat and you can't give them their money back. And if you leave them behind they will certainly die.

You cast your mind over the ten people:

Pat White   — that's you.

                              Bob White   — your brother.

          Mary White,   aged 39, your brother Bob's
                           wife. She has been ill and is still
                           too weak to eat properly.

          Tom White,   aged 19, Bob and Mary's son.
                           He's strong and helpful but,
                           unlike his father, he is rather
                           frightened of water and boats
                           and can't swim.

Donald Brown,   an engineer aged 26 and his
                 wife,

          Helen Brown,   a nurse aged 24, now seven
                           months pregnant. The Browns
                           also paid for

Jenny Black   who is Helen's mother. She is
                 active and healthy but, sadly,
                 she can hardly see, because she
                 was nearly blinded in a bomb
                 attack in the war.

Sally Scarlet,   your girlfriend, 21 years old, a
                 night club dancer. She will bring
                 her boss from the night club,

Rex Green.   He paid for Sally and has
                 promised that he will help all the
                 survivors with money when they
                 reach safety across the sea. He's
                 very overweight and drinks too
                 much.

The last person is Rex's son,   Terry Green.
He is 22, an experienced sailor
and well-known as a strong man
and a good fighter. You are
afraid that Sally admires him a
bit too much.

All these people will arrive at the beach at 10.45 p.m. in three groups: the Whites, the Browns with Jenny Black, the Greens with Sally Scarlet.

Here are some points for you to consider before you make your decision. Whatever you decide, remember that you have to leave the beach quietly tonight — you don't know how near the enemy may be.

1 Make a list of the people you really need on the boat.

2 Which people are of no use to you on the boat? List them separately.

3 Do the people you named in your first list have friends or relations among the people you named in the second one? Will this cause any problems?

4 If you and your brother are quite sure who to leave behind, decide how you can get these people to stay behind quietly.

5 What can you do if you and your brother don't agree on who to leave behind?

6 Is there any way to solve this problem without telling lies or cheating or killing people?

7 Anyway, in the end, when there are eight people (or fewer than eight if you decide to leave more than two behind) in your small, overloaded fishing boat with an old engine, what are your chances of surviving? Do you expect to escape alive?

11 CLOTH AND CLOTHES

Clothes are usually made from cloth (but of course a real fur jacket or a real leather coat is made directly from animal skins).

To make cloth (or fabric), <u>fibres</u> are spun into <u>threads</u>, which are woven together. (A fibre is defined as a material which has a length at least 100 times its diameter or width.) In the past, the weaving was done on hand looms, which are often still used by craft workers. However, most commercial weaving is now done on machines in factories.

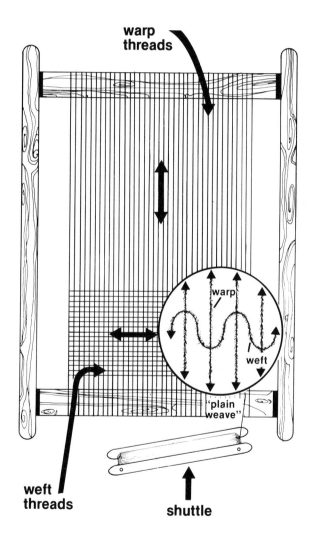

Before 1891, all the fibres used were natural; that is, they came from plants or animals. Since that date, many synthetic (or man-made) fibres have been developed.

Natural fibres can be separated into three broad categories according to their origin:

Animal: wool (sheep)
            hair and fur (camel, rabbit, beaver, mink, seal etc)
            silk (caterpillar)

Vegetable: cotton
            flax (often made into linen)
            jute
            natural rubber

Mineral: asbestos

Man-made fibres can also be divided into 'families' (according to their chemical composition):

Cellulose: rayon (trademarks eg Vincel, Durafil)
            acetates (Tricel, Dicel)

Synthetic: nylon (Celon, Bri-Nylon)
            polyester (Terylene, Crimplene)
            acrylic (Acrilan, Courtelle)
            polyurethane (Lycra)

Mineral: (eg glass fibre)

Clothes labels

As clothes are now often made from a mixture of fibres, the label on a garment should show how much (as a percentage) of each fibre is in the finished cloth. For example, a raincoat label may look like this:

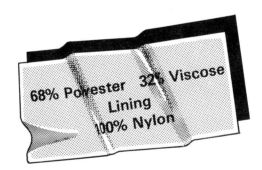

Check the labels in your own clothes to find out what fibres, or blends of fibres, are used.

Wool is an extremely useful and adaptable fibre. If you want to feel comfortable and look good, it has few equals. Like the acetates, it can be made into light or heavy fabrics, and like virtually all the man-made fibres, it dyes easily and well.

Wool is also excellent for warmth in cold weather, but if you want to stay cool in summer, it is best to wear cotton or rayon and avoid either wool or materials such as Bri-Nylon or Acrilan. Staying on the subject of weather, wool has the advantage over other fibres that it naturally absorbs moisture.

It is very important to consider the flame-resisting properties of clothing and of fabrics for household uses such as covers for furniture or curtains. If your nightdress is made from rayon, check that it has been treated; otherwise, it will burn rapidly if set alight. Some other fabrics will not burn, but will melt, and this can cause bad burns to skin; those made from acetate, nylon and polyester come into this category. Asbestos, the best-known fibre protection against fire, holds various other health hazards, and has been banned from use in clothing in the USA since 1972.

The best way to avoid damage to silk or woollen garments by moths or insects is to keep them clean, but despite this they may still suffer attacks. Most man-made fibres (with the exception of rayon, which needs to be specially treated) have a built-in resistance to both these menaces.

Static electricity can build up easily in some fibres, making the fabric cling to a person's body or giving them mild electric shocks. Synthetic fibres are particularly likely to do this, and other man-made fibres also gather static to a lesser extent. Rubber, obviously, is an insulation against electricity, but is impractical for most clothing and domestic uses.

If you can afford it, though, one particular fabric beats them all for sheer beauty: silk. As long as it is not subjected to rough wear, its glossy, ultra-smooth appearance and feel give this (frequently brilliantly-dyed) material first place in terms of luxury. Its main disadvantage, which it has in common with real fur or leather, is its comparatively great cost. When you consider that it is produced by a tiny caterpillar which has to be used by the million to make a very small amount of fibre, this is perhaps not so surprising.

Thus it can be seen that every fibre, natural or man-made, has its particular uses and characteristics, its own advantages and disadvantages. Make a table listing these, using the headings given below and the information in the passage. If you can fill in any of the blanks from your own knowledge of cloth and clothes, then do so.

Name of fibre	Man-made or natural?	Advantages/Disadvantages

Many garments are now labelled using an international set of symbols to indicate how they should be cleaned; an outline of these symbols is shown here. If you have time, try to discover which of the fabrics we have discussed in this passage need special care and should be labelled in this way.

| for washing (by hand or machine) | for bleaching | for ironing | for dry cleaning | for drying |

12   REPAIRS BUDGET

A family of four have bought very cheaply an old cottage in beautiful countryside. It was cheap because it needs a lot of repairs before they can live in it comfortably. However, after they have paid for the cottage they have only £2,000 left, so they have to choose very carefully what repairs they can afford to have done now.

Here are the most important extracts from the surveyor's report on the cottage:

```
Roof, walls, external doors in good condition.
Dwelling consists of two storeys.  Lower storey
at present contains two rooms only : kitchen
and living-room.  Kitchen is, however, large
enough for conversion into two rooms : kitchen
and bathroom.
Plans for this conversion already exist.
Kitchen has one cold water tap, one sink and
drain.  Kitchen is also fitted with electric
light and cooker (cooker out of order).
Living-room has broken cement floor, large
open fireplace and chimney.  Chimney front
is cracked and will let smoke enter room.
Neither living-room nor kitchen has any
ceiling; wooden rafters will let smoke rise
to upper storey.
Stairs to upper storey are dangerous
(woodworm).  Upper floor has two bedrooms,
both with dangerous floorboards (woodworm).
A lavatory, in working order, is in a small
shed in the garden.  The garden is large and
wild and full of rubbish and weeds.  A line
of tall, very old trees between the house
and public road should be cut down - several
trees dangerous.
```

As well as the surveyor's report they have their own drawing of the cottage on which they have marked the problem points.

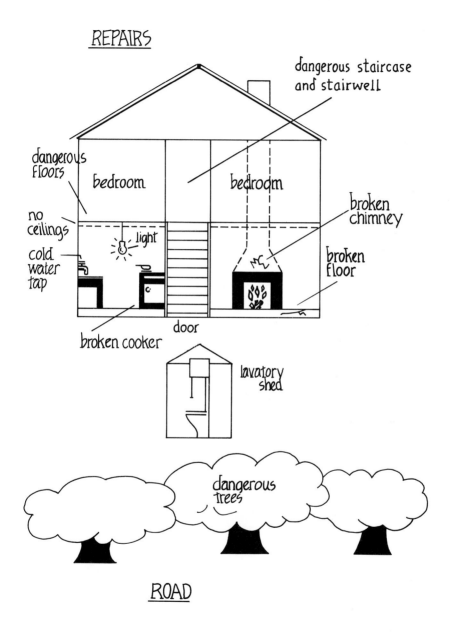

REPAIRS

dangerous staircase and stairwell

dangerous floors

bedroom

bedroom

broken chimney

no ceilings

light

cold water tap

broken floor

broken cooker

door

lavatory shed

dangerous trees

ROAD

Now, here is their suggestions list of all the repairs they would *like* to make to the cottage before they move to live there. They must keep inside their budget of £2,000.

How would you advise them to spend the money? Which are the important repairs which they must have done — or have you any other ideas?

Convert part of the kitchen into a bathroom with bath, basin
and lavatory £1,700
Repair the chimney front and check fireplace and
chimney £1,200
Cut down the dangerous trees £100
Repair all floorboards £400
Replace ceilings in all rooms £800
Treat all wood to kill woodworm £500
Mend the electric cooker £60
Mend the cement floor £200
Replace the stairs £400
Paint and decorate all walls £200
Extend electric light to other rooms £300

One of the four has also noted down these ideas:

Buy garden tools and seeds £100
Go to evening classes in woodwork £40
Buy warm winter clothes and waterproof boots £60

Decide on your repairs and your reasons for them. What could you do cheaply yourself? How will you heat the cottage? cook? see at night? wash yourself? wash your clothes?

Some useful hints that will start you thinking:

to cut down the trees will provide wood for the fire.
it's possible to cook, and heat water, over a fire.
learning woodwork may save money later.
planting vegetable seeds may save you money later on food.

Would you like to live in this cottage? Why? or why not?

13　IRON AND STEEL

We obtain most of our iron from the *iron ores*, the minerals haematite and magnetite, which are found in many places in the world, and can easily be mined. Iron ore is burnt with coke and limestone in a blast furnace. This burning produces liquid iron. The liquid iron is poured into *moulds* (shaped containers, sometimes called *pigs*) and when it becomes cold, hard and set it is called *pig-iron* or *cast iron.*

Burning coke, limestone and iron ore in a furnace also produces a waste substance called *slag* which can be used for making cement and concrete, and as a fertilizer to make plants grow (because it contains phosphorus).

Iron has some disadvantages. It rusts easily (red iron oxide is produced on surfaces because of the action of moisture) and it is rather brittle. In 1856, Bessemer devised a method of making steel from iron. Steel is stronger and easier to work with.

Steel is iron with most of the carbon removed. Air is blasted through the molten (liquid) iron so most of the carbon forms carbon dioxide with the oxygen in the air.

Steel alloys can be made if other elements are added to the steel. If manganese is added, the steel becomes much harder. (Manganese steel is used for bank safes.) If nickel and chrome are added, we get stainless steel such as we use for cutlery. And tungsten, silicon, or cobalt steels are used to make magnets.

Using this information, draw the block diagrams which follow, filling in the empty boxes with:

the materials — what we use
the products — what we make/produce
the processes — making/producing/using

1

	are mined from the earth
materials	process

2

	+		+	
material		material		material

are burned together in a blast furnace
process

3

	is poured into moulds and when set becomes	
material	process	product

4

	(a by-product of iron-making), is used in producing	
material	process	product

	+	
product		product

5

	is blasted by air to remove carbon, and becomes	
material	process	product

6

	is added to		to produce
material	process	material	process

	which can be made into	bank safes
product	process	product

7

	+		can be added to	
material		material	process	material

to produce	stainless steel
process	product

8

tungsten, silicon or cobalt		steel	
material	process	material	process

magnets
product

After you have done this exercise and checked to make sure that your answers are correct, use the information on the block diagram which follows to describe the process of refining crude oil.

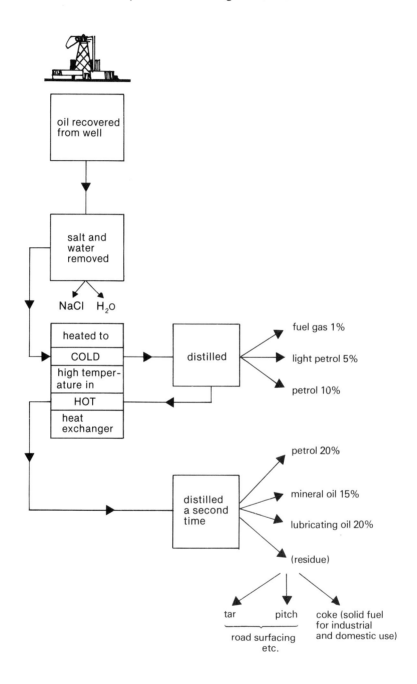

14   THE LIFE-CYCLE OF THE BILHARZIA WORM

These parasitic worms are found in Africa, Arabia and Iraq, but are most common in Egypt. Their life-cycle is complex and has many stages.

At one stage, the swimming worms live in water, usually in a dirty canal. The next stage involves a human being; if he walks or swims in the water, or drinks it, the worms can enter his body. They can be swallowed, or pierce his skin. Either way, when they are in his bloodstream they swim to an area of the body below the liver. Here they grow for about six weeks until they are adult; then the males and females mate.

After mating they swim in the bloodstream, and near the bladder or the rectum, the female lays eggs. Each egg has a sharp spine, which helps to pierce a way into the bladder or rectum. Then the eggs can pass out of the body — either in the urine from the bladder or in the faeces from the rectum.

For the next stage in the life-cycle, the urine or faeces must fall into water in which certain kinds of water-snail live — for example, into a dirty canal. Then the eggs hatch. The worms must find a water-snail, and pierce its skin. Inside its body they grow larger, and they leave its dying body as worms that can swim freely and live in water — until they enter a human body, and the cycle goes on.

This process causes various symptoms in the human carrier; these range from coughing, fever, and painful swelling of the liver in the early stages, to bleeding in the stomach or bladder, and often the creation of growths in the lungs, brain or other organs. In particularly severe cases, death can result.

To break the life-cycle and destroy the worms, there are several possible actions:

1 People who show symptoms of bilharzia can be given drugs.

2 Dirty canals can be drained and cleaned out, or filled with chemicals which will kill the snails.

3 People can be educated to understand the dangers of going into dirty water, or drinking it.

Probably the easiest way to show the life of the bilharzia worm is on a cycle-diagram. Here is a list of the stages, but not in the right order. Decide on the order. Then fit the ten stages onto a cycle-diagram such as the one illustrated here. (Of course, it doesn't matter where you start.)

STAGES

worms enter human's bloodstream
adult worms mate
worms leave dying snail
female lays eggs near bladder or rectum
urine or faeces enter water
tiny worms enter water-snail
worms grow near liver
eggs hatch in dirty water
worms swim in dirty water
eggs leave human in urine or faeces

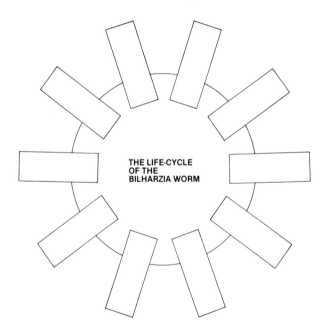

THE LIFE-CYCLE OF THE BILHARZIA WORM

Further questions on bilharzia.

1 If you were a medical officer in a country with bilharzia, which method do you think would be the best to destroy the disease?

2 Write down some advice, very simply, for people who live in danger of getting the disease; for example, take account of those people whose only source of income is from working in canals, up to their knees in infected water.

And now, here is another cycle-diagram, this time giving the stages in the life of a butterfly. Starting at a suitable point, write a short passage to explain the sequence of events.

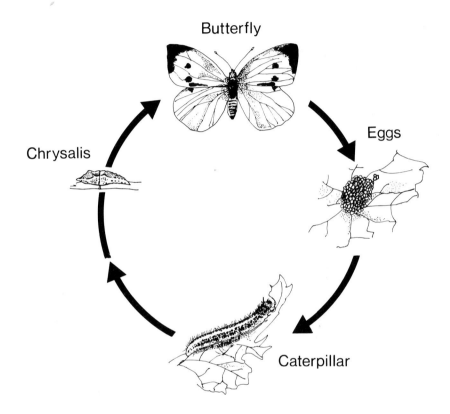

Butterfly

Eggs

Chrysalis

Caterpillar

15   ROADS IN WINTER

My friend invited me to his home for Christmas and began to draw me a map to show the different routes from Newcastle, the city where I live, to his farm at Sheephills. He was called away suddenly and I had to complete the map from what I knew of the area.

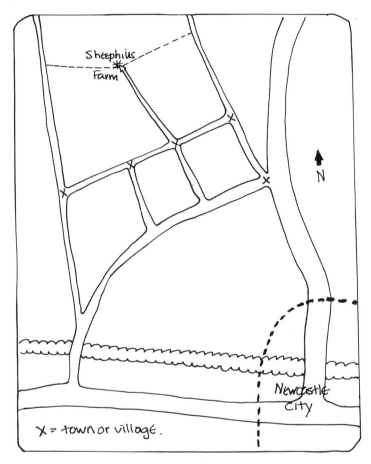

Two major roads leave Newcastle, the A31 going north and the A26 going west. The A26 runs parallel to the river Fludd. All the other roads in the area are B (minor) roads, the most important one being the B127 which leaves the A26, crosses the Fludd, and joins the A31 at the town of Coomb Major. The triangular area bounded by the Fludd, the B127 and the A31 is all planted with forest trees.

The B229 leaves the B127 just north of the river and continues north; west of the B229 is wild, hilly country. There are two other roads to mention — the B943 running roughly from east to west, almost parallel to the B127, and the B407 running north-west from Coomb Major. The B407 has a junction with the B943 at Coomb Minor.

The B943 connects four small villages, one at each of its junctions. From west to east they are: Coldhills, Vale, Dale and Coomb Minor. A rough, single-track road runs from Dale to Sheephills Farm. Sheephills can also be reached by footpaths: one joins the B229 and the other joins the B407. My friend drew them on the map as broken lines like this:

Now copy the map out and mark on it as I did:

* the A31, the A26, the river Fludd
* the B127, the B229, the B407, the B943
* Coomb Major, Coomb Minor, Coldhills, Dale, Vale
* the footpaths
* mark the forest area with trees
* mark the hilly area

So, I had a good map to plan my route to Sheephills for Christmas. The weather, unfortunately, was terrible — snow, ice and high winds — but I had a good car, a pair of skis and all the equipment I needed. Nobody wants to spend Christmas alone, so I was determined to reach Sheephills if I could.

I got as much information as I could about the weather from three different sources so that I could plan my route carefully.

Firstly, the local television news:

''Now we have pictures of the accident on the A31 between Newcastle and Coomb Major. Three cars and a lorry are involved, and icy roads and deep snow have made it difficult for police and ambulances to reach them. Motorists are advised to use other roads.''

Next, the news on our local radio station:

''Forests north of the Fludd have been badly damaged by gale force winds. Two large trees have fallen across the B127 road, just east of its junction with the B229. The B229 is open as far as Coldhills, but beyond the village the road is blocked by deep snow.''

Lastly, I 'phoned my friend at Sheephills who said:

''We're looking forward to seeing you, if you can get here. Trouble is, the snow is coming from the western hills and it's blocked the road from Dale to the farm. But both our footpaths are safe if you have skis. And local people say the B407 and the B943 as far as Vale are safe if you drive very carefully and slowly.''

Well, I had a lovely Christmas with my friends at Sheephills. How did I get there? Mark on your map one of the routes I could still have taken.

16   METHODS OF GRINDING GRAIN

Since earliest times, men have gathered wheat and other grains and ground them into flour which can be made into bread. The process of grinding (or milling) the grain has been gradually improved by the development of different equipment and different sources of power.

Early man did not mill grain, he crushed it. He would lay the grain on a large, flat stone with a natural hollow, and pound (or hit) it with a smaller stone. The resulting flour was probably not at all fine; teeth in the skulls of Stone Age men show signs of wear and damage caused by primitive bread which, no doubt, contained bits of stone and uncrushed grain.

 After the pounding stone came the saddle quern. This consisted of a broad, curved under-stone, and a long upper-stone which was rolled backwards and forwards over the grain on the under-stone. We know this method was used by the ancient Egyptians, and that slave girls worked the mills. It is a method which used the arm and shoulder muscles very heavily.

The next step was the use of rotary millstones. These were two thick discs of stone, about 35-50 cm. in diameter, 15-20 cm. thick, one lying on top of the other. The under-stone had a hollow in the centre from which a spindle projected; this passed through a hole in the centre of the upper-stone. The hole was about 8 cm. in diameter, large enough for grain to pass through as the upper millstone was turned (by a handle fixed into the stone). These mills were used from as early as 100 BC, and were still used for home milling in some places till this century.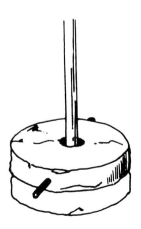

Watermills and windmills came later. The method of grinding was the same — the grain was laid between two stones — but the source of power was no longer human muscles. In the earliest watermills, the wheel was laid horizontally in the water. Later, the Romans developed the vertically set wheel. By 1086, we know there were 6,000 watermills in the southern half of Britain. Windmills are not recorded in Britain until a century later. (The idea of the windmill may have reached Britain and Holland from Persia.)

In the second half of the nineteenth century, roller mills were invented. Steam power was first used for roller mills, and later electricity. Roller milling is quite different from stone milling. Whereas stone milling only crushes the grain, in roller milling the grain is broken open, its starchy part is separated from the bran (outer part), and is quickly changed into fine flour. This makes bread very different from the bread which broke Stone Age man's teeth — but some people claim that twentieth-century factory-made bread is too refined and has lost some of its food value. For people who are concerned about this, it is possible to buy stone-milled flour, and even to buy small hand-operated mills to grind one's own flour.

Some of the information from this passage can be laid out in table form. Make your own table, using the passage, and setting out the facts under the headings given below. Not every method has information on advantages and disadvantages; in such cases, write 'No information' or try to imagine what the difficulties *might* be.

Method name	People using method/ at what period of time	Equipment used	Source of power

Description of method (briefly)	Advantages or disadvantages of method

17 THE MAYAN SYSTEM OF NUMBERS

The Maya people of Central America had a great and powerful civilisation before Europeans went to America. There are still Mayans living in Mexico, Guatemala, Belize, Honduras and El Salvador, but their civilisation is now known mainly from the ruined remains of ancient buildings. There is also some evidence of their drawing, writing and system of numbers.

Their number system in the years between about 300 and 900 AD was very different from the one brought to them by Europeans. The following series of numbers gives an example of this.

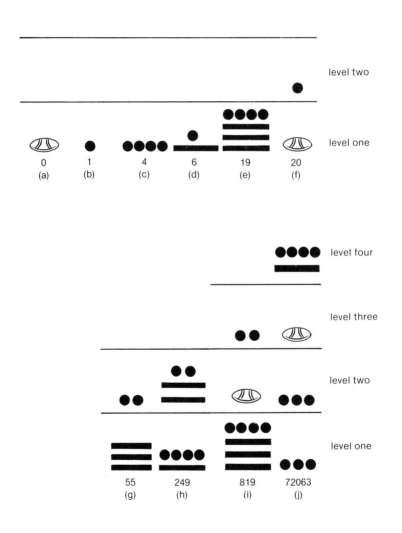

The system worked like this:

1 They had three signs: shell, ▬▬▬ bar, ● dot.

It is thought that merchants in the market place used three different kinds of beans for these signs, and set them out on the ground to calculate their accounts.

2 The values of these signs get higher depending on what level they are on. Level one is the lowest, level four is the highest (that we are considering here).

3   ●   on level one = 1,   ●   on level two = 20

   ▬▬▬ on level two = 100,   ▬▬▬ on level three = 2000

That is, on each level a sign is 20 times greater in value than on the level below it.

(So what is   ●   on level three and level four?

and what is ▬▬▬ on level one and level four?)

But   , on every level, = 0 (zero).

4 Once you have worked out the part of the total on each level, all levels must be added together.

5 With this information, check that you understand the examples (a) to (j).

Practice examples:

Write down the value of these Mayan numbers:

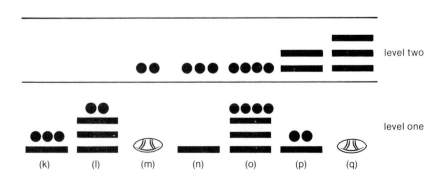

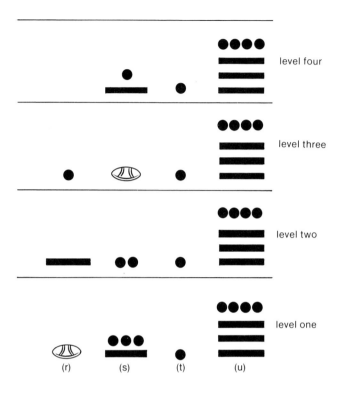

level four

level three

level two

level one

(r)   (s)   (t)   (u)

Write down these numbers in Maya signs:

(v)15; (w) 49; (x) 555; your own age.

(y) You have been using two different number systems. Fill in the spaces in the comparison of them which follows:

Whereas the Mayan system has 1_____signs only, our system has ten. Maya signs get higher in value 2_____, but ours get higher in value from right to left (eg 249 = 9 units, 4 tens, 2 hundreds). While our signs get higher by a multiple of ten, Mayan signs 3_____.

(z) Explain any *other* number system you know, for example, Roman numbers or Chinese. Try and contrast them with your *usual* number system, using the sentence patterns in (y) above.

$$2+2 = |\omega| = 7 = \triangle = |V = 8 = C = \mathcal{R} = 4$$

18 CANAL LOCKS

Canals are man-made waterways which can be used by boats and barges. Many were constructed in Britain in the eighteenth and early nineteenth centuries. On level land, construction was simpler than on hilly land. But locks were built so that boats and barges could be taken high up into hills or even mountains.

A lock consists of two watergates, the top one higher up the stream than the bottom one. Both watergates have sluices that can be opened and closed so that the water can enter or leave the pound. The pound is the area between the two gates.

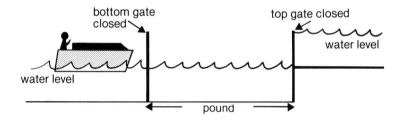

A boatman going uphill opens the sluices of the bottom gate. This lowers the level of the water in the pound. Then he opens the gate and puts his boat into the pound. The bottom gate and its sluice must now be closed.

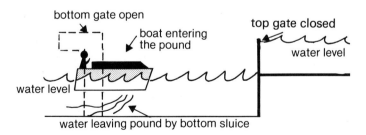

Next, he opens the sluice of the top gate. This lets the water flow in from above, and his boat will float to the level of the water above.

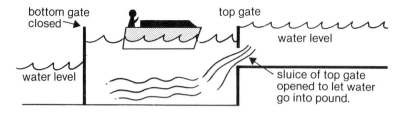

When it is at the right level, he opens the top gate and takes his boat through.

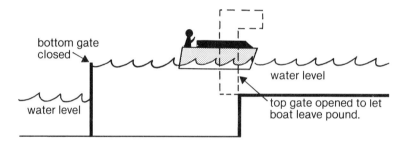

Going downhill simply reverses this process.

Task: The boatman in the diagram below wants to continue downhill along the canal. Draw a series of diagrams to show what you think he must do. Label the diagrams clearly to explain what is happening.

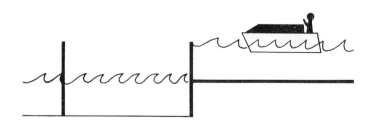

ANSWERS

1   Hardness

1 (a) diamond
   (b) borazon
2 (d) easily broken
3 (a) A fingernail is harder than wax
   (b) Steel is softer than diamond
   (c) Diamond is softer than borazon
4 (a) Window glass . . . has a hardness value of between 5 and 6
   (b) An old coin . . . has a hardness value of between 2 and 3
5 (b)
6 hard/hardness; strong/strength; soft/softness
7 (a) true
   (b) true
   (c) true
8 resists

2   The Size of Your Shoes

1 For sizes 3, 7 and (children's) 12 there are *two* equivalent Continental sizes, so
   they don't know exactly which one they need.
2 1½
3 You can get into American E, but they would be a bit too loose.
4 4
5 Hank Carter needs 10½ or 11, width 8
   Marilyn Carter needs 4, width A
   Junior needs 11 (children's)
6 49 cm.

3   Matching Partners

Mary and Richard are badly matched

(a) from Richard's point of view because:
     1 Mary is older than he requested
     2 Mary is American
     3 Mary is too tall
     4 Mary is not slim
     5 Mary is not fair
     6 Mary doesn't want more children
     7 Mary smokes
     8 Mary is not a quiet, home-loving woman

(b) from Mary's point of view because:
     1 Richard isn't a big man
     2 Richard wants four children
     3 Richard has no car
     4 Richard does not share her social interests (or her political
        or religious ideas)

4   Noise

A   5
B   4
C   1 =
D   3
E   1 =
F   6
G   40
H   70
I   40
J   100
K   90
L   70
M   10
N   30
O   120
P, Q, R   The range is very wide, and there are many possible answers to these three questions

5   The Prisoner's Dilemma

1   The best possible result is really exile (but some people might say that they would prefer to stay in their own country, even in a concentration camp; and many would dislike the thought of being used as propaganda to get other innocent people to confess to crimes they didn't commit).
2   Both must confess.
3   You get tortured, he goes free.
4   The second-best result is to go to the work camp (but some people might say exile); torture is to be avoided at all costs. Neither must confess.
5   You go free, he gets tortured.
6   Not really. Maybe you could confess, to get free, and not care about his being tortured. But you don't know — maybe he'll confess too, so you both go free; but then again, maybe he won't . . .
7   If you believe in always telling the truth, you can't confess (because you have done nothing). But you risk being tortured or sent to a work camp.
8   *That's* the dilemma!

6   The Age of the Population

1   90. No, there are few people over 90, and the pyramid has to stop at some point like this.
2   In 1891, less than 1% were over 85, and more than 12% were under 5.
3   There were *far* more young children.
4   Greater.
5   Smaller.
6   In 1891 it was children under 5; in 1971 it was children aged 5 to 10. The age groups are not very different in *age*. However, they are different in *size* — the 1891 largest group is about 12%, the 1971 largest group is about 8%.
7   People between 15 and 65 are the working population — and this group includes parents, too, who can greatly affect the future pattern of the population pyramid.
8   In 1891, 15 to 20; in 1971, 20 to 25.

The answers to the final questions will depend very much on your country and its economy, technology, medicine and religion.

7 Murder

The following are the simplest answers, with the most obvious murderer. If you think this is too simple, choose a different person as the murderer and work out how he/she could have done it.

1 Colin's two lies are:
(a) he says he never visits his aunt, but Bob says they visited her on the day of the murder (so *one* of them is lying).
(b) he says he was watching 'Monster Movie' at 7.30, but Dan says it began at 7.40, and Emma says she saw him at 7.35 (so someone is lying).
2 Dan is probably lying to his mother, not the police — because he went to Emma's house after the movie so he was late home.
3 Colin is the obvious one (but try the others); he got the poison from Alan's chemist's shop; he said he was at the cinema watching 'Monster Movie'.
4 Colin could have got the poison in Alan's shop, when Alan went out for a few minutes (but so could Bob).
5 That afternoon, Colin went to ask his aunt for money — she refused. He went to Alan's shop to borrow money — Alan refused. He stole poison from the shop. Sometime before 7.30 (we don't know exactly when) he entered his aunt's house and put poison in the milk. He was in the streets at about 7.35 when Dan and Emma passed him on their way to the cinema. Probably he went to 'Monster Movie' so he would know its story, thinking that it would give him an alibi.

(But try explaining the day spent by Alan, Bob or Dan, and see if they could have done it).

8 Crop Rotation

FIRST YEAR

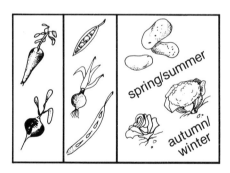

SECOND YEAR

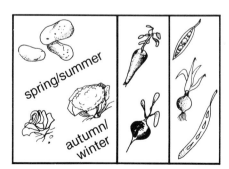

THIRD YEAR

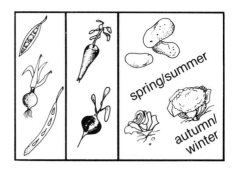

FOURTH YEAR

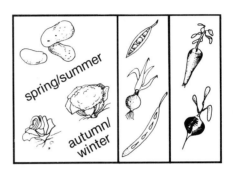

<u>DON'T</u> grow this year's greens in the same place as last year's greens!
<u>CHANGE</u> the positions of your crops because
1 You will need less fertilizer
2 The plants are less likely to get any diseases
3 The pests won't increase in number.
Follow our successful crop-rotation plan!

9 Identifying Animal Tracks

From top to bottom:
otter, cat, badger, weasel, dog, fox.

10 A Place in the Boat

1,2,3 There is no satisfactory answer — every group contains useful people
and dependent people
4 You'll have to change your plan and leave early. But the other people may not
trust you — they may be there early too!
5 You'll have to go very much earlier — or kill him?
6 Probably not
7 Probably not

Name of fibre:	wool	cotton	acetate	rayon	nylon	polyester	asbestos	silk	rubber	acrylic	polyurethane	fur	leather
man-made	−	−	+	+	+	+	−	−	+	+	+	+	−
natural	+	+	−	−	−	−	+	+	+	−	−	+	+
comfortable	+	+						+					
attractive	+							+					
light and heavy fabrics	+		+										
available in many colours	+		+	+	+	+		+	+	+	+		
warm in winter	+												
cool in summer	−	+			+	−				−			
moisture-absorbent	+												
comparatively expensive	−	−	−	−	−	−	−	+	−	−	−	+	+
gathers static	+		+	+	+	+			−	+	+		
attacked by moths etc.	+	−	+	−	−			+	−	−	−		
fire-resistant		(∗)	−	(∗)	(∗)	+							

∗ − do not *burn,* do *melt.*

NB: Only that information which it is possible to gather from the passage is inserted here.

12 **Repairs Budget**

There are no set answers to this problem. There are many possible and sensible ways of spending £2,000 on repairs.

13 Iron and Steel

1 *Materials* — iron ores *or* haematite and magnetite
2 *Materials* — iron ore, coke, limestone
3 *Material* — liquid iron; *product* — pig-iron *or* cast iron
4 *Material* — slag; *products* — cement, concrete, fertilizer
5 *Material* — iron (molten *or* liquid iron); *product* — steel
6 *Material* — manganese; *material* — steel; *product* — manganese steel
  (*or* harder steel)
7 *Materials* — nickel, chrome, steel
8 *Process* — can be added to (*or* are added to); *process* — to produce
  (*or* to make)

14 The Life-Cycle of the Bilharzia Worm

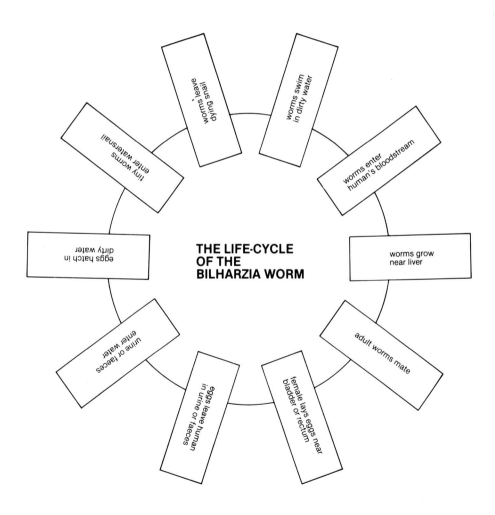

THE LIFE-CYCLE
OF THE
BILHARZIA WORM

worms swim in dirty water

worms enter human's bloodstream

worms grow near liver

adult worms mate

female lays eggs near bladder or rectum

eggs leave human in urine or faeces

urine or faeces enter water

eggs hatch in dirty water

tiny worms enter watersnail

worms leave dying snail

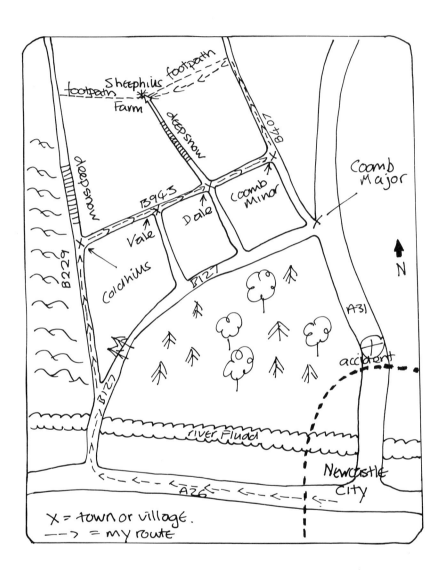

Sheephills footpath

footpath   Sheephills
              Farm

deepsnow

B407

Coomb
Major

deepsnow

B943

Coomb
Minor

B229

Vale

Dale

Colchills

B127

N

A31

accident

river Fludd

B127

Newcastle
City

A26

X = town or village.
---> = my route

Method name	People using method/ at what period of time	Equipment used	Source of power	Description of method (briefly)	Advantages or disadvantages of method
rotary millstones	from as early as 100 BC, and some still used until this century	2 disc-shaped stones. Under-stone had a spindle. Upper-stone had a central hole, and handle	muscle (plus use of handle)	upper-stone was turned by handle; grain fell through hole, and was ground as stone moved	no information
watermills	Romans developed vertically set wheel	1. mill building; millstones; wheel set horizontally in water 2. mill building; millstones; wheel set vertically in water	water	similar to rotary millstones, but worked by water	no information — but better than early methods
windmills	recorded in twelfth century in Britain; the idea may have come from Persia	mill building with sails to catch the wind; millstones	wind	as above, but worked by wind power	no information — but better than early methods
roller milling	invented in the second half of the nineteenth century	large, mechanically driven rollers in factory	1. steam 2. elec-tricity	rollers break the grain open, separate the starch from the bran	it makes fine flour, but may lose some of the food value

3   ●   on level three = 400

   ●   on level four = 8000

   ▬▬   on level one = 5

   ▬▬   on level four = 40000

Practice examples:
(k) 8   (l) 17   (m) 40   (n) 65   (o) 99   (p) 207   (q) 300
(r) 500   (s) 48048   (t) 8421   (u) 159999

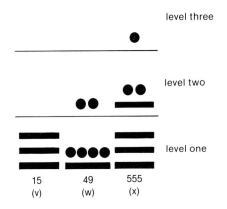

level three

level two

level one

15   49   555
(v)   (w)   (x)

(y)   1 = three
     2 = from the bottom to the top of a page
     3 = get higher by a multiple of twenty.

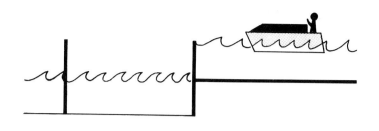

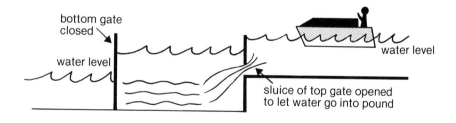

bottom gate
closed

top gate
closed

water level

water level

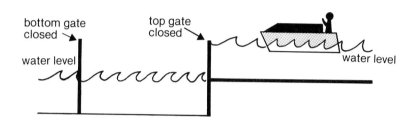

bottom gate
closed

water level

water level

sluice of top gate opened
to let water go into pound

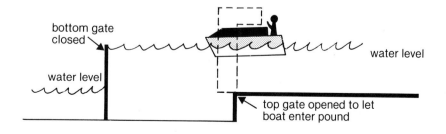

bottom gate
closed

water level

water level

top gate opened to let
boat enter pound

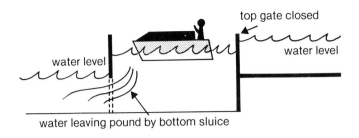

top gate closed

water level

water level

water leaving pound by bottom sluice

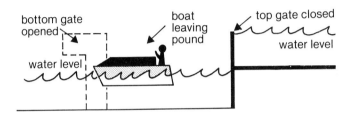

bottom gate opened

boat leaving pound

top gate closed

water level

water level

Printed in England by E. J. ARNOLD & SON LIMITED, Leeds